Private School

It's Not Just for the Wealthy Anymore

A Parent's Guide to Getting Your
Child Accepted into Private School

Sandra L. Frazier

A Better Tomorrow Publishing
UPPER MARLBORO, MARYLAND

First printing 2008

ISBN 978-0-9795768-0-5
LCCN 2007903158
Library of Congress Cataloging in Publication Data is available.

Editing, design and production coordination by
About Books, Inc.; www.about-books.com

This book is dedicated to parents throughout the country who want to reach out to enhance the lives of their children.

ACKNOWLEDGMENTS

Thanks to my children, Dominic and Micah, for being so cooperative in the process of looking for new schools. In addition, thanks to my parents, Franklin and Julia, and my brother Ron, who helped me with revisions to the book. Thanks to John for watching over things when I was working on this project. Thanks to my best friends, Janice and Lionel, and to my family for listening to my school stories with interest and suggestions.

CONTENTS

PREFACE

Have you ever thought about putting your child in a private school but concluded you could not afford the tuition? Do you currently have your child in a private school but feel that school is not satisfying all your needs? Do you want to change schools but need some help with the process? If so, the information in this book on the process of applying for private schools will inform you of your options.

This book will guide you through the process of applying to private schools. I hope it will come as a welcome source of information for you and will clear up any misconceptions. Contrary to what many people believe, private school is actually available for people with a variety of incomes. Even if your household income is modest, private school is still an option for you.

While considering the possibility of private school, think in terms of getting the best education for your child. Many private schools can certainly offer an excellent learning environment. Knowing your child and his or her goals, needs, and aptitudes is an essential part of making the right choice. Private school could well be the beginning of a new and rewarding future for your child.

INTRODUCTION

If you went to college and received financial aid, you may still be paying off student loans. If you had a child who went to college, you or your child may be paying off the student loans. Financial aid for private school is not the same as for college. For the independent school systems, financial aid comes in the form of a grant. You will not be required to make a repayment on a grant. Many religious-based private schools obtain funding through their organizations to assist people with paying part of their education expenses. So when you think about looking at a private school for your child, keep in mind that there are resources available to help fund his or her education.

Your goal is for your child to receive a great education that will provide a rich perspective on life and open the door to a successful career. If you grew up in an industrial or agricultural region during the 1940s, 1950s, or 1960s, you know the value of a good education and how it is crucial for obtaining higher-salaried jobs. The bottom line is that education is the key not only for getting a better job but also for having a better life.

Part of the reason for the current unsatisfactory situation with our public schools is that our world has been transformed by technology and new global industries, but our school systems have not changed. Public schools still teach the same three "Rs", reading, writing, and arithmetic, in the traditional way, without teaching children how to apply the lessons to today's world. Sure, we put computers in classrooms and teach children how to use them; however, we have not taught children to think any differently or how to apply the information they learn to their lives and their future.

Private schools are not regulated in the same way as public schools and so are able to be more progressive in their approach to education. Private schools are still required to teach certain subjects to maintain their accreditation, but for many private schools, the techniques used to teach these subjects have been enhanced to adjust to our ever-changing world.

Children who attend private schools are exposed to many things and opportunities that so many children are not exposed to in public schools. Some of the enrichment programs offered to older children in private schools allow them to travel overseas. In religious schools, many children conduct missionary work in other countries. Children who attend private school tend to see more of the world outside of their local neighborhoods and so acquire an enlarged perspective on life.

Community service is an important part of a private education. Sometimes children help build a structure in a community or work on a farm, at a nursing home, or in a shelter. Children in private schools learn to respect all types of people, environments, and situations from various experiences. Children are also taught teamwork and how to depend on each other to complete projects. Some schools teach students how to overcome obstacles at an early age through projects. Learning these concepts as a young child has a huge impact, because as an adult, your son or daughter will be able to adapt and think on his or her feet.

While I was looking for a school for my daughter, someone asked why I would invest in education for a small child. Another person asked my friend if it is worth it to send a young child to private school. My answer is yes, because during my research I found that many private schools have a process to their education that is not available at public schools. Many private schools combine themes throughout their curriculum to keep the flow of learning consistent regardless of the subject. Consistency helps children grasp concepts more easily. If the theme is bumblebees, the children learn about bumblebees in science, use bumblebees to count or multiply in math, read about bumblebees in English classes, and so forth.

Previewing a new school will be an eye-opening experience for your child. You will find that every school you visit may not be the right choice for you and your child, but you may be able to walk away with a concept or an idea that you would like to use in your child's everyday life.

If your child is already prepared academically and mentally to go a private school when you start looking at schools, this book will provide the steps to the process of admission. If your child is not yet prepared academically or mentally, this book will guide you through the process to get him or her there.

The next step after private high school is college for most students. Many colleges start recruiting children in private school during ninth and tenth grades. In the public school system most recruiters come to schools during the eleventh and twelfth grades. Being exposed to recruiters earlier, in the ninth and tenth grades, and taking tours at college campuses during summer breaks will change a child's perspective on his or her future because he or she will be able to visualize it. The experience of staying at a dormitory, going to a few classes, and experiencing what college life can be like is transforming. Most children who are given that exposure will want to go to college after that experience. So a child's desire to perform well in schools increases.

Additionally, children who perform well academically at school will increase their scholarship opportunities. The majority of children who go to private schools and do well academically are offered scholarships to college. In addition, children who attend some private middle schools and perform well academically are offered scholarships to attend private high schools.

We have to look at new ways to guide our children's education. Education is not the end; it is just the beginning. If education exposes our children to more of the world, the doors that will be opened to them will be endless. The exposure your child receives to people and events can make his or her life greater than you could ever have imagined. The opportunity is there for all who choose to go after it.

No one knows what the future is going to hold, but we must change because change itself, in the world around us, is constant. Most private schools are changing with the times and adapting to society. We need to have our children in an environment where they can grow and change with the world.

PART 1

Preparing Your Child

—◆—

If you are reading this book, then you are probably prepared to take more control over your child's education. By finding the school that is right for your child, you are going to give him or her something no one can take away: an education that will enrich the rest of your child's life and that will have great practical value. Whether you are pregnant or have a toddler or a child already enrolled in school, this book will walk you through the necessary steps to prepare your child for entering private school. The beginning, no matter what age your child is now, is the most important part of the work.

Your Involvement in Your Child's Life

When considering putting your child in private school, think about what your child really does well. Is your child a person who does well with hands-on processes? Is your child an auditory person who performs tasks well after having a one-on-one conversation? What activity does your child excel at that you have done together? Keep that thought in mind when you look at what a private school has to offer. There are lots of schools to choose from, so you want to select a school that is a good fit for your child.

How have you prepared your child for school? This question is not about any type of formal training. Just think about your involvement in teaching your child various tasks. Most private schools are looking at more than academics. They are looking at the whole child in terms of interests or hobbies as well as the child's family and family involvement.

At the toddler stage, what are you teaching—or what did you teach—your child? Most children learn through playing. Have you taught your child how to paint or write his or her name? Or perhaps you have taught your child to hit a baseball or a golf ball. Does your child like to run in the grass, make mud pies, or mold playdough into creative shapes? Perhaps your child likes to watch *Wheel of Fortune* or some other TV shows. Some children like to talk. Do you have conversations with your child and read to your child? If so, you are already preparing a great learner.

If not, start working with your child now. It is never too late to be involved in your child's life. Most children want to learn. Most young children are eager to learn most anything. When my son was four years old, I taught him how to add and subtract numbers. When he was five, I taught him multiplication. He loved math, so I focused on math.

Summer Learning

Many states have adopted a year-round school operation in which children go to school throughout the year. Most schools, however, still offer the standard three-month summer vacation for students, a tradition rooted in America's agricultural past. Keeping your child engaged in learning through the summer is part of the process of preparing your child for academic success. It also helps ensure that your child will not lose the information he or she learned during school. Many stores offer workbooks that provide activities for children based on their grade in school. Depending on your child, give him or her a set number of assignments each day based on your child's learning style. Also prepare some type of reading activity for your child.

There are three basic leaning styles: visual, aural/auditory, and kinesthetic. In other words, individuals tend to learn best through their eyes, their ears, *or* their bodies. Most children and adults learn best by a combination of two or all three of these styles, but one style is usually most efficient. Most children have a great need to be in perpetual motion until about age eight, which can make identifying a preschooler's learning style a challenge. It is never too early, however, to begin watching your child and discovering all you can about his or her thinking.

You may have an auditory learner if your child is quick to notice sounds, talks a lot, is good at explaining, and enjoys acting/performing. If your child is an auditory thinker, get audio books, better known as books on tape, for him or her. Most libraries have a good selection of books on tape and CD in the children's section. You and your child can listen to a book on the way to the store or at any other outing. Your child can also listen to a book at home while doing his or her chores or some other activity. For auditory learners, it will be helpful to repeat the instructions or information you give him or her multiple times.

If your child tends to like complex ideas and tasks, he or she may be a visual-spatial thinker. Since visual-spatial thinkers usually learn best from visual displays, engage your child with activities that use a lot of print, color, graphics, posters, and maps. Activities can include putting puzzles together, drawing, music lessons, playing computer games, and tracing letters, numbers, and words. Using flashcards to learn is also helpful for visual learners.

Researchers have found that some visual-spatial thinkers have difficulty with finishing tasks and sometimes have poor listening skills. If this is true for your child, find ways to bring him or her back around to finishing the puzzle or game after a break. Also, repeat the instructions or information you give your child multiple times. It may also help to write things or tasks down so your child can see them often. Most children want to comply with your instructions; however, they may forget and need to be reminded. Researchers have also found it is helpful to keep visual thinkers away from fluorescent lights.

Your child may be a kinesthetic or tactile learner if he or she needs hands-on activities that help make abstract concepts concrete. Kinesthetic people learn best by doing. These children are easy to spot because they are always moving, enjoy sports and action, like to build, and seem to want to touch everything.

One strategy you can use if your child is a kinesthetic learner is to give him or her hands-on projects. Making hand puppets using a paper bag and then drawing a face on the bag and playing with the puppet is an example of a short, interactive hands-on project. When your child is drawing, put music on that he or she likes to hear. If your child is coloring or drawing, let him or her use a bed or the floor as a desk. One of the best things you can do is let your child discover something through any type of adventure. Keep your child's activities short and active. Kinesthetic people perform better when allowed to take frequent breaks.

Television Time versus Toy and Reading Time

How much television does your child watch daily? If you haven't already considered limiting the amount of television your child watches, please consider it. Set a scheduled amount of television time during the school week. A fair suggestion is one hour of television per day. Your child will quickly learn to make good choices in selecting his or her television programs. Most people who adopt limits find that when the child's television time is over, he or she will play with toys, read a magazine or book, or play outside of the house. Children quickly learn to make good use of their time. You may also find that your child will devote his or her time to an interest or hobby.

Interests and Hobbies

What are your child's interests or hobbies? The reason hobbies are relevant and important in this context is private schools want to know that your child is well-rounded and has extra-curricular interests; they also want to know about your involvement in those interests and that you play an active role in your child's development.

If your child hasn't yet taken up a hobby, introduce him or her to one. The hobby or interest could be checkers, Scrabble, chess, marbles, painting, reading, writing, playing an instrument, model building, collecting stamps or coins, birding, martial arts, civil air patrol, gymnastics, cheerleading, or something else. There are a great number of choices for hobbies. The only criterion for choosing one is that the hobby or interest must suit your child.

Many of these activities or interests can be pursued through your local community center or YMCA. Many local community centers have a schedule of activities in which you may already have participated. If you are looking for an interest or hobby for your child, your local community center or YMCA is a place to start. If you haven't already participated in an activity, sign up for one that fits into your schedule or the schedule of a friend or family member who can take your child to the community center. Just make sure it's something your child will like.

Book Clubs

Have you ever considered starting a book club with some of the neighborhood children? It is an inexpensive way to get children interested in reading. You do not have to pay for books if you use the library. You can meet at the library and have each child select a book he or she wants to read. Before the children select their books, tell them to make sure there are enough copies for the other children. After they make their selections, sit down as a group and decide which book to read first. Then make a list of the other books so that each child knows his or her book will be read.

You and the children will create the rules of the book club. You can decide what day the children will meet. The main rule should be how much needs to be read before the next meeting. The book club should decide if it is a chapter, a certain number of pages, etc. At each meeting, the club will discuss the book as a group.

If this is your first time being in a book club, you may want to get a book on tape for the first meeting. The club members can listen to one chapter of the book together. After they listen to the chapter, have a discussion about it. If these are young children, you may have to probe them with questions like, What do you think is going to happen next? or Who is your favorite character so far? Ask questions to gain an understanding of their interpretation of the book. It is also a good idea to have a snack at the meeting. The process of discussing each chapter as a group after hearing it will be very helpful for subsequent meetings when the children have to read their chapter or pages on their own.

In any type of club, expect attention spans to be limited by the age group. Also expect that children will learn in different ways and at different levels, so you will need to monitor their progress and adjust your club expectations as needed. For instance, in a book club there may be a child who didn't read all or any of the chapter. The other children are very likely going to blast the child who didn't complete his or her assigned reading. Bring the other child along by having the children give a summary of the chapter, and ask the child to start the next chapter along with the others. A child who, for whatever reasons, could not read part of the book will more than likely not be able to catch up after falling behind. Try to keep that child engaged in the group. This lesson is good for all of the children in the group because it teaches forgiveness and how to be helpful.

If your lifestyle doesn't include time for a book club, consider subscribing to *Highlights Magazine* or *Highlights High Five* for children who are not old enough to read. Another children's magazine is *National Geographic's Kids* or *Little Kids Magazine*. These magazines have stories, activities, riddles, mazes, and puzzles that you and your children can enjoy together.

Having hobbies or interests does not have to be expensive or fabulous. It just needs to be something that your children do and enjoy.

Checker or Chess Clubs

Starting a checker or chess club is inexpensive as well. If you find one person who knows how to play chess, that person can teach all the children how to play. The children who pick up on the game quickly will automatically start teaching other children. The beauty of learning chess is that children become strategic thinkers and begin to think beyond their immediate moment into their future.

All that is needed to start a chess or checker club are a few chess or checker boards that each child can bring to the agreed-upon place. These games are inexpensive, and they can be purchased at a local store or in a consignment shop or thrift shop. You may also have a neighbor who would be willing to share with your children a chess or checker set that is not being used. With any club, the group needs an agreed-upon meeting place and a commitment. The commitment from the children doesn't need to be anything complicated; there just needs to be a consensus among the children on when they can meet and how long they will play.

Golf Clubs

Golf is another hobby or sport that doesn't have to be expensive. There is a program called "The First Tee" at many golf courses. It costs about $50 for the year to join. The First Tee program teaches children from ages six to seventeen how to hit a golf ball and how to putt. Children go to the golf course once a week for a lesson. If your time permits, you can take or have your child taken to the driving range at the golf course as many times a week as possible. The First Tee program gives the children a ball card to receive a free bucket of golf balls to hit every day. If you don't have any golf clubs, contact your local golf course and find out if they have any golf clubs that can be borrowed or purchased for a low price. You can also find golf clubs in your local *Penny Saver*, newspaper, consignment shops, or thrift shops.

Of course, there are many other sorts of clubs and activities your child could become involved in; these are just a few examples.

What Schools Are Looking for in Your Child and Your Family

When you begin looking at private schools and find some potentially interesting candidates, have a conversation with your child about your thoughts for a new school (if he or she is old enough to understand the situation). The key element in being accepted to a private school is your child. Your child has to be an active participant in the acceptance process. A child is like anyone else: He or she needs to know what is going on and how the change in school will impact his or her life. There may be something your child wants to learn but hasn't asked about because the opportunity doesn't exist at the school he or she is currently attending. Your child may ask you to find a school that has a chorus because he or she loves to sing at church or a school that offers lessons for a particular musical instrument or teaches Chinese. You may be both delighted and surprised at what your child is interested in learning. Whatever his or her interest, encourage it, and let your child know you will pursue it.

I talked to my son during his fifth-grade year about changing schools, but he did not want to change. He was comfortable with his current school, and he liked his environment. His arguments against changing schools were that he was making good grades and had a lot of friends and fun at school.

PART 2

What Do You Want from a Private School?

Why are you looking for a private school for your child? Is it the academics? Is the current school not providing enough of an academic challenge? Is the current school really giving your child a well-rounded education? My decision to move my child to a new school was based on academic challenge. Even if your child is making good grades, you should not be deterred from looking at a private school. Good grades, after all, do not necessarily equate with good education. All children need to be challenged to their fullest potential.

Most people find that going through the process of applying for school opens up their children's eyes to a larger universe of possibilities. The schools the children see may be quite different from their current schools. There may be separate libraries for lower, middle, and high school. Libraries may have big, comfortable chairs and fireplaces, creating an inviting environment for reading. There may be separate buildings for middle and high school. There could be a music room with all types of instruments. Community service, digital photography, and digital art may be offered. There could be differences in the class schedules. The school may have breaks scheduled in the day for children to go and relax or hang out.

The concept of having a different environment may change your child's perspective on going to a new school. Bear in mind that through the process your child may revert back to his or her original mindset and resist change. As an adult, you are probably aware that change is not easily managed in most adult situations involving work, home, and relationships. As adults, we realize that change can be scary, so be mindful that for a child change can be twice as scary. The best way to introduce a change is to have constant communication. Anyone can adapt to change if he or she is aware of the process that gets him or her to a new venture in life. As a parent, you are in the driver seat throughout this process, so you will have to drive the decision. Just be sure to do so with sensitivity to the child's point of view.

Knowing when to start looking is important to the process. If you are looking for admission to a private school, you need to start in the early fall months. The admission decision letters to a private school are mailed in March for the next year. If there are more qualified applicants than the school has spaces to fill, then there are usually waiting lists as spaces become available.

Academics

For many people like you, the attraction of private schools is not that they are private. Many of us want our children to go to private schools because they are supposed to provide a great academic education, which will give our children a leg up in life. The other side of the coin is that your child needs to be successful academically to be accepted to the school in the first place.

Reviewing Your Child's Present Academic Status

If you want to put your child in a private school, take a look at his or her report cards for the last two years. Did your child have mostly A's and B's? If not, take this time to work with your child on getting his or her grade point average higher over the next year. Talk to your child about what subjects he or she likes. If your child likes bugs, find out how you can make science a better experience for you child. Take your child to your local museum. The Smithsonian Institute in Washington, D.C., has museums with all types of scientific bug displays. Many museums, like the Museum of Science and Industry (MOSI) in Tampa, Florida, and the Franklin Institute Science Museum in Philadelphia, Pennsylvania, have interactive scientific displays. Children love to play at interactive museums, and many museums don't charge a fee for these activities. Call your local museum to learn more or search for information on the Internet.

Take some time to find out what your child doesn't like. If your child doesn't like handwriting, find out why. Has your child learned to hold a pencil comfortably? If your child doesn't like English, find out whether he or she has yet grasped subject-verb agreement or any other grammatical topic that might be posing problems. You may find that most of the things children don't like are more what they don't understand than true innate dislikes. If you help your child grasp a crucial concept, he or she may learn to like the subject.

Is your child bored at school? Perhaps he or she can do the work and do it well but isn't motivated because there's no real challenge. If that is your situation, talk to teachers to find out whether additional responsibilities can be assigned to your child. Sometimes children just need one more push to become interested in a subject.

If you have a child who is at the entry age for school, pre-kindergarten, or kindergarten, private schools are obviously not going to require transcripts or teacher recommendations. Private schools are going to get a reference from a daycare provider or a preschool teacher. The questions schools ask concern such things as whether your child can share with others, whether your child is imaginative, curious, and creative, and whether he or she can think and act independently. Take a look at the website of the elementary school you are thinking about for your child and look at the daycare questionnaire. If there are topics on that questionnaire on which your child will not be judged favorably today, work on getting your child up to speed now so that when it is time to ask for a daycare referral, the referral will be positive.

The Role of Parents in Education

Your current school provides part of your child's education, but as parents, we all need to play a part in the learning process. We need to review our children's homework. Parents, I caution you that review means just that—review their work. Parents who do the homework for their children are not helping them. Eventually, those children will not be able to perform at school the way their homework shows they can. Teachers are also keenly aware of the difference between the writing style and maturity of thought of children and adults. At a meeting I attended last year, one teacher spoke about parents doing homework for children. Ironically, she noted that the parents were consistently making grammatical errors that she had previously corrected in class.

When reviewing your child's homework, if you don't think the answers are correct, go over the concept that he or she is learning in school. If your child still feels lost or if you don't feel qualified to help with the particular topic, set up a meeting with the teacher to get extra help with the subject matter. If your work schedule doesn't allow you to go to the school, set up a telephone conference with the teacher in the evening. If that is not an option, ask a friend or family member to help you with the situation or have your child work with another child who has grasped the subject matter. You might also be able to find useful information on the Internet. Be creative in getting the help your child needs to understand a concept or process.

Supplemental Learning Programs

There are many programs that can help sustain, enrich, or augment your child's progress in such subjects as reading, math, and writing. Many learning centers focus on test preparations as well. The Sylvan Learning Center, for instance, offers a tutoring service in writing, reading, and math. It offers online tutoring as well as face-to-face tutoring. Sylvan can tutor by grade or by subject. Sylvan's process is to identify the child's unique strengths and needs; then, Sylvan develops a customized tutoring plan just for your child, providing individual attention. You also get progress reports every step of the way. Regardless of whether your child needs tutoring to catch up, keep up, or get ahead, Sylvan Learning Center may be your best choice. The website for Sylvan Learning Center is http://tutoring.sylvanlearning.com/index.cfm.

C2 Educational Centers were founded on the belief that every student deserves the best instruction possible. They specialize in academic tutoring and counseling and have helped countless students do better in school. C2Educators work with students of all ages and needs, whether it is for remediation, maintenance, or enrichment. The website for C2Educate is http://www.c2educate.com/.

SCORE! Educational Centers have been providing kids with a fun way to catch up, keep up, and get ahead in their studies. *SCORE!* works with children in grades pre-K through 10th grade to help them achieve their goals and reach their academic potential in math, reading, spelling, and writing. Their programs include personal academic coaching, positive reinforcement, and a customized curriculum that adapts to each child's pace and learning needs. The website for *SCORE!* Educational Centers is http://www.escore.com.

Huntington Learning Centers help children with supplemental instruction in reading, writing, mathematics, study skills, phonics, and related areas. Their website is http://www.huntingtonlearning.com/.

Another program is Kumon. The premise of Kumon is that children learn by repetition. Children are assigned worksheets to complete each day. The subjects Kumon offers are reading and math. Each subject takes about fifteen to twenty minutes a day. Children who work through Kumon's worksheets will not just memorize the information for a test and then forget it.

Kumon eliminates some of the fears children have about taking tests because through repetition they become secure in their knowledge of the subject. The reading portion of Kumon teaches not only subject-verb agreement, vocabulary, and general grammar but also comprehension. Kumon teaches how to get the main idea out of a paragraph.

The Kumon process is to test children first to find out what level of work they can comfortably perform. Kumon's approach is to build confidence in a child by having him or her master the level of work he or she can achieve at first. Once a child masters a level, he or she is tested. If a child passes the test, he or she goes on to the next level. The idea is also to get the child's knowledge beyond his or her current grade level. If a child has seen a concept before he or she sees it in a school classroom, the fear of something unfamiliar is eliminated. This boosts a child's confidence and ensures he or she can do the required work. Your child may not get all the answers correct on a test, but he or she will not give up because the fear has been eliminated.

Be aware, though, that if you engage your child in a program such as Kumon, you have a part to play. You need to take ten minutes of your day to check your child's work. The Kumon Center will give you an answer book for each subject your child takes. Your responsibility is just to open the answer book and check your child's work. There is a simple process to be followed. You indicate which answers are correct, and if any answers are incorrect, you simply put a checkmark next to the number of that question. You then return the work to your child for correction. If his or her corrections are still not correct, you place another checkmark next to it and put the worksheet in the box to be returned to the Kumon Center on your next visit.

This process takes away the need to try to instruct your child. It eliminates guilt from the child, and it eliminates anger from the parents. When the Kumon instructor reviews your child's work, he or she will take the time needed to instruct your child on the correct process for getting to the right answer. The Kumon approach to learning is inviting to children because Kumon offers an enhancement to their learning. There is no stigma attached to receiving this kind of help in advancing to the next grade level.

Most people go to the Kumon Center twice a week, selecting days that fit their schedules. Children attend classes and do their work on days when they go to Kumon. When they leave, they get enough work to last until their next visit, depending on their schedule for that particular week. A child can start Kumon as young as two-and-a-half years old. Check with your local Kumon Center for information; the website is www.kumon.com.

For any learning center, check the Internet to find a location near you and to get information on the cost of each subject per month. If your budget is not ready for supplemental learning and you really want to give it a try, ask for help. You may be surprised that a family member, co-worker, or friend may want to sponsor your child for a period of time.

Children with Learning Challenges

If your child has learning challenges or difficulties, there are organizations that offer help. Schwablearning.org offers a free service that both identifies the learning difficulty and provides help with getting your child on track. For more information, go to the organization's website at www.schwablearning.org.

There are probably other learning centers in your area, either on a local or national operational level. If you think your child can benefit from a learning center, you need to shop and compare to find one that fits him or her. Check www.ask.com or www.google.com to search on your specific question.

Tutoring

There are also many other ways to enhance your child's learning. Many colleges offer tutoring gratis or close to it. The "No Child Left Behind Federal Program" has many companies and schools competing for students because the federal dollar will fund their tutoring programs. In turn, your child can be tutored at no cost. The U.S. Department of Education oversees this program under the Supplemental Education Services tutoring program. As of 2007, the accountability to monitor the program lies with each state. That may change if states do not make the necessary changes to get qualified children into the programs. If you are interested in getting tutoring through this avenue for your child, check with your local Board of Education to see what services are available.

Also, if your local college has an education program, more than likely part of its curriculum is student teaching. Student teaching sometimes comes in the form of tutoring. College students get credit for tutoring children. Also, some Parent-Teacher Associations (PTA) have programs that enrich learning. Some of those programs include tutoring. To find out what is available to you, contact your local school Board of Education. Any program can be effective and have positive long-term results.

A tutoring service may be your choice. No one method works for all children, and no one method is better than any other. Consistency in your method of choice is the best way to accomplish your goal.

The Parent-Teacher Relationship

Your commitment to your child's current school also plays a part in the process of applying to a new school. If you have open communication with teachers, they will respond favorably to requests from you to add additional classroom responsibility or to provide additional challenges to your child's workload or to work with your child on enhancing a skill set for a particular subject. Open communication does not mean that you have to attend every Parent-Teacher Association meeting or that you have to be the homeroom parent. Your communication with the teacher can be achieved through the passing of notes through your children on various subjects and setting up conference calls or meetings as needed. You will also benefit by sending a "thank you" note to your child's teacher when he or she has gone above the call of duty to assist your child with personal needs.

Do you or your spouse ever have to travel for your job? If so, send letters to your child's teacher to let him or her know when you will be out of town and who will be caring for your child. This lets the teacher know that if your child's behavior is a little erratic, it is probably because he or she is missing you at that moment. Most children are creatures of habit, and when the habit is changed, the child may react differently. Because teachers are with our children for seven to eight hours a day, keeping them updated on your child's home life will help them to understand atypical behavior. Keeping teachers informed also lets them know you respect them and are aware that they may be with your child more than you are with your child.

Recognition of a teacher on teacher appreciation day or when the teacher steps out of the box and does special things for your child goes a long way toward getting the extra help or attention your child needs.

No matter who you are or where your child attends school, there are going to be some problems. I had a situation where my son broke his right index finger. He had a brace for three weeks. He struggled with learning to write with his left hand. Even though a brace is obvious, some teachers will not be sensitive to such a change. I had a teacher rip up my son's homework because he wrote with a pencil rather than a pen. My son was upset about getting a zero on his homework, but he was more fearful about upsetting the teacher, so he begged me not to say anything. I spoke to the teacher about the situation at a parent-teacher meeting. The teacher said she was not going to give my child a zero, but she wanted to teach him a lesson about using a pencil.

When speaking to the people who spend most of their day with your child, be gracious. If at all possible, you do not want to have a serious confrontation with a person who will be guiding your child the next day. With the broken finger situation, I held my tongue in terms of my emotions; however, I told the teacher she did a good job of scaring my child and that my child used a pencil because he did not write well with his left hand. After the parent-teacher meeting, I spoke to a few other mothers I had not seen in a while and was on my way out the door when the teacher approached me again. She began asking questions about how long the brace would be on and started thinking of ways my son could complete his assignments without actually having to write them out. The situation was turned into a win for my son.

What I found really interesting about my son's reaction to my having a conversation with his teacher about the incident was the anxiety he experienced. He was not able to go to sleep before I came home from the meeting. He approached me when I came home from the meeting with a heavy heart, hoping I didn't speak to the teacher about the situation. I told my son that I had spoken to his teacher. When he asked me what I had said, I simply told him that tomorrow he would be fine. I told him there was nothing for him to worry about and that nothing else needs to be said about that homework assignment. I did not share the details of my conversation with the teacher with him. When I came home from work the next day and asked my son about his day, as I always do, he said his day was great.

Children don't need to know the particulars of any conversation you have with a teacher. They only need to know any special instructions that emerge as a result of a teacher conference.

PART 3

Choosing Schools

When choosing a school, take a look at your current school environment. What do you like about the current school? What do you want to see in the next school? Is it Advanced Placement (AP) courses to give your child a head start in college? Is it the sports or science program? Technology? Facilities? Extracurricular opportunities? There may be other factors. For instance, many religious schools have a great deal to offer in terms of morals, values, and academics. Depending on your religion, you may be looking at religious schools to determine a good fit for your child and your family.

Whether you choose to pursue admission to an independent or religious school, there is a process to follow. If you have access to the Internet, use it to obtain a lot of information very quickly. Most schools have websites where you can search by name. You can also access www.privatebug.org/, which lists all private schools in the United States. You simply need to pick a state and a city, and you will get a listing of schools.

For independent schools, the website is www.nais.org/. This website has a locator that will give you options to search for schools by city, state, religious affiliation, sports programs, special programs, and types of schools (e.g., day or boarding).

Comparing Schools

Another website to review is http://yahooed.greatschools.net/content/schoolChoiceCenter.page. This website provides information about how to research and compare schools. It also has information about making the choice between private and public schools. There are a lot of great public schools in our country. In some areas, there is a lottery process to getting into those schools. Some public schools are called magnet schools. They provide programs that promote equity, diversity, and academic excellence for all students in public school choice programs. If you are interested in public schools that offer a more robust curriculum, you can go to the Internet and do a search on magnet schools to find one in your area.

Again, knowing your child is the key to determining which schools to pursue. Things to consider include:

- Day school or boarding school
- Religious or nonsectarian school
- Co-educational environment or single-sex environment

Many single-sex schools are paired with another school of the opposite sex. The thought process behind having a single-sex school is that children are not preoccupied with the opposite sex while attending their daily classes. Being paired with another school gives the children the opportunity to interact with the opposite sex for extracurricular activities such as plays, chorus, sports, and community service.

Once you select the criteria you want to pursue, the Internet can help you find a listing of appropriate schools. Additional information on the list includes the earliest entry grade, the highest entry grade, and the school's location. The independent school website also provides information on the number of students enrolled as well as any special programs, summer programs, and information on languages they teach. There is a link to each school's website, so you can begin looking up information on any particular school.

Some schools stop after third grade. These schools have an affiliation with other schools that start at fourth grade. This may be a new concept for you if you are familiar with elementary schools that go from kindergarten through fifth or sixth grade.

You can begin your search by going to each school's website and looking at its admission process. All websites have an admissions link and provide an overview or welcome to the school. They also have a link to the application process. The websites provide information on specific dates in terms of the age cutoff for your child as well as what are the best entry-level years.

Student Ages—How Old Must Your Child Be to Enter School?

The age cutoff for your child will be different for private schools depending on birth months. Most public schools will accept your child as long as he or she turns the specified age before November or December of that school year. Private schools have different birthday cutoff months for admissions. Some schools have a birthday cutoff of September 1st. Some schools want your child to be the appropriate age plus four months. If your child is entering pre-kindergarten, for example, he or she will need to be four and four months old by September 1st to qualify for applying to the school.

Even if the private school you are applying for has an age cutoff at September 1st, many of the schools feel that children born in May and the summer months are young for their programs. Don't let this information deter you from applying if your child was born in the May through August months. You know your child and his or her capabilities. Also, if your child is in a structured pre-kindergarten or daycare at three or four years of age, your child may be mature enough to get into the school of your choice.

Here is an example of *entry-level years* for a school that starts at fourth grade and goes through twelfth. Entry-level years are:

- fourth grade for lower school
- sixth or seventh grade for middle school
- ninth grade for high school

The school starts at fourth grade, so it will probably be accepting sixty to eighty students as fourth graders for the next academic year. This doesn't mean your child could not be accepted to the school if he or she were entering at the fifth grade. The entry-level years just let you know when there are the most available spaces to enter school. Usually, the school will add an additional class at the middle and high school levels, so there will be more spaces for entry at sixth, seventh, and ninth grades. Entry level at those grades may be only for one new class, which is usually between fifteen and twenty students.

Every school is going to lose some students during the year or at the end of the year through natural attrition as people relocate or leave the school for other reasons. Keep the entry-level years in mind because they hold the most openings each year. Other grades may have only three or four openings available, so the competition is stiffer.

When you are looking at entering private school at the middle or high school level, there will be approximately fifteen to twenty openings at the entry-level years. This doesn't mean all new students will be in those grades. Schools will integrate new students with the existing students; however, these schools strive to keep their class sizes low. Schools may only allow for the number of students to fill one additional class with some attrition based on the re-enrollment of their existing students.

The Admissions Calendar—Keep up with the Dates

Most schools will provide an admissions calendar that supplies information on each month's events. For example, November will probably indicate that open houses are being held on certain dates. December and January calendars may indicate that applications are being accepted or that tours are being scheduled at that time.

School admissions links on the websites may also provide you with the information on the application forms that will need to be completed. Most of the websites have applications forms that are in a PDF file format. If you don't have an Adobe Acrobat reader on your computer, go to one that does so you can download the forms. If that is not an option for you, contact the school to obtain the forms. The cost of admissions should be included on the website. If the cost is an issue, don't let that stop you from applying. Some schools will indicate a reduced fee if you're applying for financial aid or indicate that you can contact them for a fee waiver.

The website may also provide you with some helpful lists of frequently asked questions (FAQ). The websites also list key contacts, providing both email addresses and phone numbers.

Other People's Opinions—Sometimes It Is Good to Hear What Others Think

Another piece of information you may find helpful is the opinions of parents who have had children at the school. A website called "great schools" has parent reviews for the various schools. Go to the website http://yahooed.greatschools.net/modperl/parents/dc/185/ to get a parent review on the school. The only critiques are those of the parents who have left statements. The information is as true as the perception of the person who wrote it. If there are multiple opinions, you can see where there are consistencies or inconsistencies.

As you go down your list of schools, make a note by the schools you want to consider and mark through the schools that are not a good match for your child. Transportation is discussed in another chapter, but if the only disqualifier for a particular school is the location, bear in mind that the school may provide transportation for your child.

Creating a List of Schools to Pursue

After you go through all the schools, you need to put together a list of ones you want to visit. If you are requesting information in writing from the school, then label and set aside manila folders for the information you are expecting to receive. If you are printing information off the Internet, put the information in a folder and label it for that school. Keep all of your school information in one place. It could be a large bag, a file cabinet, or a cardboard box. Just keep it together. You will find that you will reference and compare the information frequently.

You might be thinking, why would I need a list of schools? Why wouldn't I just pick the one school I want and pursue it? That approach is certainly an option. If you are the type of person who can make a decision based on what you have read, seen, and/or heard about a school, then that approach is what you should pursue. Bear in mind that the grade level your child is applying for will have a limited number of openings.

Depending on your geographical area and the grade level your child is applying for, the ratio of acceptance can be anywhere from two to one to twenty thousand to one. If you are willing to take a chance that you will be able to obtain that one position, then you only need to apply to the one school you want.

Perhaps you can look at the process of applying for schools the same way you would look at the process of applying for a job. If you are in the market for a new job, you are going to apply to the jobs you feel you are qualified to handle. The rationale you would probably use is that you are increasing your odds of getting a position by applying for more than one job.

If your search begins in the spring, consider checking the summer camps the school has to offer. If you want to get a feel for the environment and staff, consider enrolling your child in summer camp for a period of time. Enrolling your child in summer camp may give you an advantage in that the school's staff will be familiar with your child by the time his or her application is reviewed.

Keeping Track of Deadlines and Dates

To keep track of the schools and the dates for applying, tours, and deadlines, it will be useful to put together a spreadsheet of all of the schools. See the sample spreadsheet on the next page.

When your spreadsheet is complete and if your child is of an age when he or she can understand the process, go over the schedule together so that your child will know which schools you are going to visit. You may want to keep a copy of the schedule at work in the event something comes up so you can call the school in advance and re-schedule. The website link enclosed in the front of this book contains access to a spreadsheet of how to document your information. There are also instructions for updating and tracking the information.

Now that you have a list of the schools you want to consider for your children, start making those telephone calls or go on their websites to set up your parent tour, interview, or open house RSVPs. Each school will be different in respect to what you can set up first.

School Dates to Remember

Sample Schedule					
Date	Time	School	Item/Process	School Code	Student
5 Oct.	10:30 A.M.	School H	Visit/Tour School H School	XXYY	Child B
23 Oct.	A.M.	School J	Call to schedule Child A's classroom visit; shoot for October 27th or Nov 3rd	XXYY13	Child A
2Nov.	8:00 A.M.	School K	Family Tour and Interview w/Child A	XXYY65	Child A
4Nov.	2:00 P.M.	School L	School L open house with Child B. Make a decision on applying.	XXYY60	Child B
8 Nov.	12:45P.M.	School M	Visit/Tour School with Child A	XXYY90	Child A
13Nov.		School M	Call to set up interview and classroom visit. Call to set up the test for January 20th (preferred) or 27th.	XXYY90	Child A
13Nov.		School K School M	Transcript and Teacher Recommendation Request submission date	XXYY65	Child A
13Nov.			ISEE—Need to schedule		Child A

The Open House—Attend As Many As You Can

An open house is a good way to see the school and its classrooms. Open house visits are usually scheduled for weekends, so you and your child can go together. Schools may use students to give family tours. Your child will get the perspective of the school from a child of the same age, which can be very helpful. Teachers will be present at the open house to provide information about the school and to answer questions, and you should also receive a packet of information.

If you decide to pursue that school, contact them to schedule a visit for you and/or your child. Each school is different. Some schools will want to meet the parent first, and some will want to meet both the parent(s) and the child together. Follow the process for that school and set up the appointment. Put that appointment on your spreadsheet. If the visit/interview is with your child, send a letter to your child's teachers to let them know your child will be arriving late or leaving early on that date. This will enable you to get the day's work and homework from your current school. See the sample letter on the next page. The website link enclosed in this book contains this saved document as well as an early dismissal letter.

Sample homework request letter for late arrival

Date: [Insert Date]

Dear [Insert Teacher's Name],

[Insert child's name] will be arriving late for school on [insert day and date]. Will you please give him/her his/her class work and homework assignments on [insert previous day]?

(If your child has a project due, you can include the following: Also, I have reviewed [insert child's name] project. Please let me know whether he/she can turn it in on [insert day] to earn extra credit.)

If you have any questions, please call me at [insert number].

Sincerely,

[Insert Your Name]

The Application Process

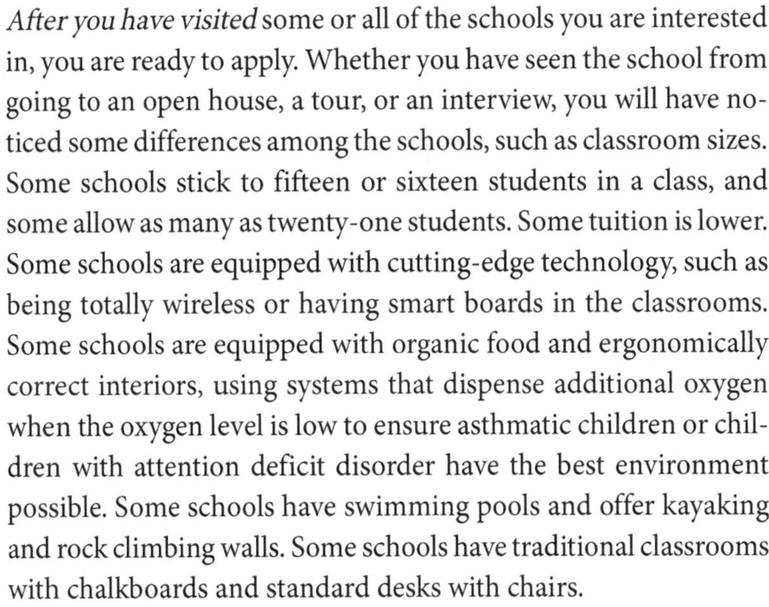

After you have visited some or all of the schools you are interested in, you are ready to apply. Whether you have seen the school from going to an open house, a tour, or an interview, you will have noticed some differences among the schools, such as classroom sizes. Some schools stick to fifteen or sixteen students in a class, and some allow as many as twenty-one students. Some tuition is lower. Some schools are equipped with cutting-edge technology, such as being totally wireless or having smart boards in the classrooms. Some schools are equipped with organic food and ergonomically correct interiors, using systems that dispense additional oxygen when the oxygen level is low to ensure asthmatic children or children with attention deficit disorder have the best environment possible. Some schools have swimming pools and offer kayaking and rock climbing walls. Some schools have traditional classrooms with chalkboards and standard desks with chairs.

Anyone shopping for a school will notice these differences—they are not subtle. While considering your school of choice, bear in mind that schools with enhanced features will cost more. The cost should not deter you from considering a school for your child. You will understand why when you get to the chapter on financial aid.

Deadlines

Each school has a deadline for its application. If you know you are going to apply, submit the application. Each school may have an application fee. If the application fee is a financial constraint for you, then ask the school if there is a waiver on the fee. Some applications may indicate the waiver information on the form. If you are applying online, you may need to call the admissions office to get the information about an application fee waiver for the online process.

For those of you who are procrastinators, I urge you to apply as soon as you know the school is a great match for your child. In addition to the application, there are other forms that need to be completed and followed-up on. Get as many papers completed as you can.

An application may ask you to answer some questions about your child or to give a parent's statement. It may ask you to describe your child, or it may ask about your child's hobbies and interests. Take some time to think about your answers. You want to respond in the most honest and positive way possible. If you are not certain about your response, ask a friend or relative to read it and give you an opinion. The person may give you some insight as to how you can clarify your response or give you a suggestion about what to add to your response. You see your child every day and so may not recognize a great quality in your child simply because you are so close to him or her.

Some schools will ask your child to provide a personal statement, write an essay, or answer a few questions. Let your child write that personal statement. You will not be helping your child by writing it for him or her. Just as teachers know when a parent has done the homework, the admissions staff will know when a parent has written a personal statement.

Review what your child has written. If he or she hasn't used the best handwriting or has misspelled words, have him or her re-write it with good handwriting and spelling corrections. That should be your only advice. These tools are helpful to schools considering your child's admission. If your child's personal statement comes in as if he or she is a college graduate, the school may have the wrong expectation or an unfavorable impression of you. Let the school know what it will be working with when your child enters its doors. Schools are there to educate your child.

Teacher Recommendations

The school is going to ask for at least two teacher recommendation forms for any child who is currently attending school. For children under four years old, a school will ask for a recommendation from a daycare provider. The school will indicate which subject they want for the teacher recommendation.

For elementary school students, the school may want the information from your child's prior year's teacher. If you have moved recently, you will want to make the connection to the prior year's teacher in a timely manner. Make the process easy for the school. Provide a stamped envelope with the school's name and address on it so the teacher or school can mail it.

Note: The return address on that envelope needs to be that of your child's school. You will not be able to mail the recommendation, nor will you be able see the recommendation that the teacher completes. If available, provide your school with a fax number to send the information. See the sample letter on the next page that can be included in your request to have your teachers complete the forms. The website link enclosed in this book contains this document.

Sample teacher recommendation request letter

Date: [Insert Date]

Dear [Insert Teacher's Name],

Will you please complete the attached form for [insert child's name]? He/she is applying for another school for next year. The school requires that if the math and English teachers are the same that the science teacher should complete this evaluation form. If you have any questions, please call me at [insert number].

Sincerely,

[Insert Your Name]

Transcripts and Test Scores

Transcripts and test scores are required by most schools. Your school may provide one or two transcripts without charge; however, there may be a charge for additional transcripts. Test scores will be from standardized tests your child takes each year. Some schools require two years' worth of test scores. See the sample letter on the next page, which can be included in your request for transcripts. The website link enclosed in this book contains this document and some variations on the document.

Sample transcript request letter

Date: [Insert Date]

Dear [Insert Registrar's Name or Office Staff],

Here is the [dollar amount] for one more transcript for [Insert child's name]. Will you please forward his/her transcripts and test results to the schools on the attached forms? I really appreciate it.

If you have any questions, please call me on [insert number].

Sincerely,

[Insert Your Name]

Some schools will ask for an optional referral from a friend. Ask a friend who knows your child well to complete the form. It is your responsibility to make sure your child's file is complete. Keep track of the dates by which you requested information on transcripts, teacher recommendations, and mailed applications. See the sample task list.

Sample Task List

Sample spreadsheet of school schedule							
School	Schedule Tour	Complete Application & Send	Application Received	Financial Aid Requested	Parent Visit	Child Visit	Transcript Requested
School A	Complete	Yes–11/13	Delivery Confirmation 11/14	Yes, with application on 11/13	Yes, 11/2 Combined w/ Child A	Extra Interview on 12/1 w/Mrs. X	Yes 11/16
School B	Complete Nancy X 555-1212	Yes–Given on 11/28	Yes, hand delivered to Mr. Mantle @ Tour	Yes, within application	Yes, 11/28	01/10 w/Mr. Elks @ 9:30 (Science)	Yes–12/1 took to My School
School C	Complete	Sent on 11/13	Yes, letter to confirm on 11/20	Yes, within application	Yes, w/Child A on 11/8	Yes, 11/30	Yes
School D	Yes–Open House	Sent on 11/27	Yes–11/27	Yes	Yes, on Dec. 6 w/Child A	Yes, 12/6 optional Shadow day is avail.	Yes–12/1 took to My School

See the complete sample spreadsheet in the website link for documenting the dates.

Once you think all of the documentation should be at the school, send an email or call the school to ensure everything has been received. Have your spreadsheet handy when you contact the school. If the school says it didn't receive a transcript, check with your child's current school to verify when it was sent. If a teacher recommendation was not received, find out what subject it was for so you can follow-up with the correct teacher. See the sample letter below. There are additional sample follow-up letters in the website link that you can use to follow up with the teacher or school registrar.

> ### Sample follow-up letter for a teacher recommendation form
>
> Date: [Insert Date]
>
> Dear [Insert Teacher's Name],
>
> Will you please complete the attached form for [insert your child's name here]? The school did not receive the original form the school sent on [insert date here]. The school needs to have the form by [insert date here]. I know this is short notice, but I just found out the school didn't receive the original teacher recommendation. I really appreciate your help.
>
> If you have any questions, please call me on [insert your phone number here].
>
> Sincerely,
>
> [Insert Your Name Here]

The Interview Process

Every school is going to want to have a conversation with your child. The school may call it a tour or an interview. For any child, it really is a conversation. I would strongly suggest you have a conversation with your child to prepare him or her for that conversation. Some schools will interview your child without having you present.

Your Child's Interview

The famous biblical quotation "out of the mouth of babes" applies to children of all ages. My son said some things that made me want to crawl under the table at one of his interviews. The admissions director asked my son what subjects he liked and which ones he didn't like. My son said he didn't like science, and the director asked why. My child's response was that it is was boring and he fell asleep in class. My mind went through a full cycle from panic, reprimand, and then recovery. I quickly interjected a question to my son that brought him around to clarity. I asked him how he maintained an "A" average in science if he had been asleep. He responded that he didn't really fall asleep but that many of his classmates did. I told him he should only respond to the questions on behalf of himself, not his classmates. I thought my son's initial response to the admissions director was the big red flag that said, "We Don't Want This One."

Preparing for the Interview

When you talk to your child, have a brief conversation instructing him or her only to respond positively. Let your child know that just because you are looking at new schools is no reason to bash or put down the current school. If your child makes a comment you perceive as a blunder, find a way to let him or her know how the question could be answered better. Afterward, change the subject. You don't want to make a big deal out of the situation. You do want to keep your child's self-esteem at a high level, and you also want to keep your child engaged in the application process. So be positive and help your child feel good about the experience.

Even though you may have worked through an interview situation, don't be surprised if you witness another blunder at another interview. At a tour we attended, my child was firing off questions to the admissions director that had either already been answered or that were redundant. When he stepped away to use the restroom, I waited a few feet back from the group. When he came out, I spoke to my child as softly as I could and instructed him not to ask another question. He looked at me as if I were out of line.

Children do not always perceive the situation the way an adult does, so don't be surprised if you need to explain to your child what appropriate behavior is more than once. Again, you need to make your point and change the subject. The goal is to preserve your child's self-esteem while you work on getting your own inner temperature under control. If you berate your child, you are going to lose in the process of finding a good school.

The conversation you have with your child prior to the interview should include practice questions. If the admissions director asks, "Why don't you like a subject," tell your child to say something that is true (e.g., "I get frustrated with new concepts, and my teacher doesn't explain them," or "I only like it when I can understand it"). This will give the admissions director a better understanding of your child's situation. Ask your child to ask only questions about things he or she really needs to know.

Instruct your child on manners and mannerisms. A child who can look an adult in the eye, focus on what is being asked, and respond coherently is not the average child. I know that behavior is what we all would like to see, but it is not typical. The best thing you can do is ask your child to try to focus on answering the questions and try not to interrupt the person asking the questions. Ask your child to try to sit up straight and try not to fidget or pick up objects from a table (e.g., a glass turtle or a porcelain vase). Just try to think ahead in order to be prepared.

You know your child, so I would caution you to advise your child accordingly. You also need to understand that he or she is a child and will do what comes naturally. If you think what comes naturally to your child is going to be a detriment to the interview process, then I suggest you coax your child by practicing the interview. A practice session will set both of you at ease.

By All Means—Feed Your Child before the Interview

Another important preparation for the interview is food. If your child is preoccupied with the fact that he or she is hungry, you can guarantee an unfocused conversation. If you are running late to the interview, make sure you bring your child a snack. That snack can be a peanut butter and jelly sandwich, some fruit, or some pretzels. Just make sure your child is not hungry. After that, all you can do is hope for the best.

The Parent Interview

The parent interview can be interesting as well. Keep in mind that you are shopping for a place that will enhance your child, house your child, and respond to your child for most of his waking hours, five days out of the week. The school that you choose and that chooses you will see your child more than you will for nine months out of the year. You want to hone in on what the school has to offer your family, and you also need to understand what an average day is going to be like for your child. You want to be comfortable with the environment. Take this opportunity to find out whether a school is a good fit for your child. The conversation you have with the school's representative should not be threatening in any way from either party. Take a look in the mirror. What do you notice about yourself when you are speaking? Are you clear in your responses? Do you come across as approachable and respectful? If you do, then the school is going to be interested in you. Teachers and administrators need parents with whom they can work and who will assist them in guiding students through various processes and activities. If you do not come across as approachable, then you need to work on your demeanor. A positive attitude will be essential for your interview.

When you go on tours and open houses, a lot of information is given in group settings. The main purpose of the parent interview is an exchange of information. You need to find out as much as you can about the school. Likewise, the school is trying to gather information about your child that it can't really get from the paperwork. Be open with the school officials about what is going on with your child. If your child was just selected for a sports team, started taking voice lessons, works at teaching a younger sibling how to do something, or is learning skateboarding, let the school know that about your child. You are selling the school on the idea that your child will be an asset. The school officials are selling you on the fact that this is a great school. You and the school are looking for a win-win outcome.

Ask questions. If the school is on a trimester schedule and you don't know what that means, find out. If the school offers a transportation program that is not clear to you, find out the particulars of the program so you can really understand how children get to school. Transportation is important and a big factor in deciding where you should apply. If the child's schedule has him or her taking some classes three days a week and other classes four days a week, find out how the rotation works.

Shadow Day—A Day for Your Child to Visit

Some schools will offer a shadow day. A shadow day gives your child the opportunity to spend the day at the school. Your son or daughter will be paired with another child, and together they will go to all of the same classes, just as though your child were attending the school. Shadowing another child gives your son or daughter the actual daily school experience and will help your child understand what an average day is like at that school. It will also help your family to decide whether that school is a good match. If your child is going to have a shadow day, use the shadow day letter from the website link to give to his or her teacher(s).

Interviews for Pre-Kindergarten and Kindergarten Children—A Play Date

For children who are going to kindergarten or pre-kindergarten, the interview is a play session. The key to making this a positive experience is talking to your child prior to the visit. Think about how your child reacts to new surroundings. Is your child clingy or exploratory? Apt to throw a tantrum if you step away or more likely to wave goodbye and start playing with toys? Some children can be either clingy or independent; it all depends on the child's mood.

Many parents don't give young children a lot of information because they have no concept of time. Young children live in the present. Many parents don't start talking to them about where they are going until they are on their way. If your young child is going to visit a school, give him or her more lead time than usual. Your child needs to get used to the idea that he or she is going to be away from you in a new setting.

On our visit to the first school we were considering, I didn't tell my daughter about it until the actual day of the visit. She did not have enough time to understand the concept of separation. She was happy to be at the school as long as I was with her. She clung to me and cried when I tried to step away. I was fortunate that the teacher was able to coax her into looking at the fish tank while I went to the parent portion of the visit. I was nervous that my child was going to be uncomfortable for that hour. When I went to pick her up, she seemed happy and was ecstatic to see me. When I asked the teacher how the visit went, she only replied that they had had fun. Well, it was over, and I knew I couldn't get the past back, so I just changed my process for the next visit.

On the day of your visit, talk to your child about the new school. Let your child know that he or she is going to be in the room with the toys and that you are still going to be at the school, just in a different room with the other parents. Your child may not want you to leave when you start explaining the process. Tell him or her you are not allowed to play with the toys, so you must go to a room where the other parents are going to talk while their children play with the toys. Tell your child you will not leave the school without him or her. Your child should understand and wave goodbye without reservation.

Testing, Testing, Testing

The age of your child has no bearing on whether he or she will be tested for entrance into a private school. All schools need to estimate your child's academic aptitude and will look at test scores and grades. They want to find the high achievers in their pool of applicants. Many private schools are also striving to create more cultural diversity in their student populations. Although testing and grades are important, there are times when diversity is used in granting entrance to schools.

Standardized tests have limitations in terms of gauging accurately the intelligence and potential of a child. Private schools are typically aware of this phenomenon, and that is why they base entrance decisions not only on test results but also on other criteria, such as grades, interviews, recommendations, writing samples, and personal information.

Grades—High Achievers Stand Out

Anyone who wants to put a son or daughter in a private school needs to make sure the child's grade point average (GPA) is at least 3.0 or higher. Every school requires a minimum GPA for admittance. Regardless of that precise number, be aware that most private schools are looking for high academic achievers.

In chapter two, I discussed supplemental learning centers and tutors. If you think your child could benefit from these types of supplements, be proactive and enroll him or her with a tutor or a learning center. As an active participant in the learning process, you will quickly be able to determine the return on your investment.

Again, you will be responsible for getting your child to the learning environment and for making sure your child does the work at home. Your interest in your child's supplemental learning will go a long way toward your child's success. Learning centers may also improve your child's test scores, as your child will be tested numerous times in his or her supplemental learning program.

Testing Pre-Kindergartners Up to Fourth Grade

For pre-kindergarteners, kindergartners, and children up to grades three or four, many independent schools require the Wechsler Intelligence Scale for Children (WPPSI) or a similar test. The WPPSI test is an individual test that does not require reading or writing. The testing facilitators ask children questions and have them perform certain tasks like building blocks or block design, picture arrangement, math questions, etc. Most of the topics are graded as pass or fail.

Many schools will provide a listing of education centers in your area that provide this test. If this type of testing is a new experience for you, you may be wondering how do you test a three- or four-year-old child? Tests are conducted as a play session where children are asked to play with blocks, puzzles, and other toys. The testing professional will ask questions and make observations of your child's behavior. You may also be curious about what type of professional is going to be conducting the test. Usually, it will be a licensed psychologist. Note that the test may be more expensive than the cost of the entrance exam for an older child. If the cost of the test is an issue for you, find out whether any waivers are available. If the center doesn't have a waiver, find out from the school you are applying for whether it has a waiver. The waiver may not pay for the entire test, but it can offset the cost.

Young children need to be prepared for the test. I prepared my child by telling her we were going to meet one of my friends and that she was going to be able to play with toys and puzzles. I told her I would be with her and would be sitting outside the playroom waiting for her. In addition, I dangled the carrot that we would go and have some fun after our visit.

When we arrived at the testing center, I was pleasantly surprised at how comfortable we were made to feel. The psychologists offered puzzles and coloring materials for my child for the first fifteen minutes while we were in the waiting area. When the psychologists came over to my child to ask her how she was doing, there was an instant connection between them. There was no pro-test from my daughter when they went into the classroom. The test took about forty-five minutes. After the test, I scheduled a follow-up visit.

The purpose of the follow-up visit is to review the test results and to read all the information to make sure you understand it before it is mailed to the schools. The results will indicate your child's age in years and months on the first page along with his or her other personal information. The rest of the information will explain the cognitive results and the criteria used to score the child. The results also discuss the verbal subtests and performance tests.

Ratings indicate how well your child scored and how he or she ranked in terms of an age equivalent.

An example of one of the verbal subtests is receptive vocabulary. Receptive vocabulary assesses a child's ability to comprehend verbal directions, and it measures the auditory memory and the integration of visual perception and auditory input. The child looks at groupings of pictures and selects the one that the tester names out loud.

The test results rank your child in a range from very superior (VS) to considerably below average (CBA). Your child's age equivalent is given for each category. An example of the age equivalent is four years, one month. Your child's actual age may well be higher or lower than the age equivalent. A percentile average is also given to show where your child falls in comparison to other children. The percentile can be anywhere from 0 to 99. The last few pages describe what the psychologist observed during the test, the test results, and a summary.

Schools that have an age cutoff at September 1st and consider children based on where their birthday falls in the year (as a young kindergartner or a mature kindergartner, based on biological months) use the information in these tests to obtain your child's true mental age.

For some of the religion-based schools, the testing is conducted at the schools. For young children, the test can be anything from how they handle separation from their parent or guardian for two hours to how they articulate words, share, manipulate puzzles, and play with toys. During the time children are being evaluated, teachers also look at the social interaction, noting how well they speak and respond to others. Some testing can include reading to children or trying to engage them in an activity that takes more than five minutes to try to determine their attention span. Some schools test dexterity to determine coordination. Testers may play a game of catch with the children or ask them to hit a ball with a bat. Each school has its own methods. Most schools know that one to two hours is not a true test of children's abilities.

Testing for Children Who Are Reading and Writing

For children from grades one to eleven, many schools require the Independent School Entrance Exam (ISEE) or the Secondary School Admissions Test (SSAT). The schools you are interested in applying for will indicate which test or tests they will accept. Most schools accept both. If any one of the schools you are applying for will only accept one, then select that test. That way, your child only has to take one test.

The independent school system has a uniform process. The testing is done one time. Your child takes one test, and the scores are sent to the schools of your choice. The way this process works is that each school is assigned a school number for testing. When you register your child for the test, enter all the schools you are applying to on the form. Registration can be done online or by mail or fax with a completed registration form. If you register online, you can find the school's number online. If you register by mail, a booklet with the school numbers will be included for you to put on the registration form. You are allowed to enter a set number of schools without an additional fee. After that, you will be charged for each additional school that needs your test scores. If the cost of the test is a concern for you, contact the school you are applying to and ask if it has a waiver for taking the test.

In addition, there may be a school on your list that requires your child to take its own individual test. It may accept the test scores from the standardized test as well. This is not the normal process, but it could occur. There probably will not be a fee involved with taking that particular school's test.

There will be about three or four different dates available to take the test. When scheduling the test, keep in mind any school deadlines for a completed application. Also keep in mind where your child is academically. I would suggest you give your child time to learn as much as possible before taking the test. The test scores are usually sent to the schools within two weeks.

Practice Testing—I Highly Recommend It

To prepare your child for the test, the testing companies publish a book of full-length practice tests. The practice guides can be ordered online, by mail, or by fax. I strongly suggest you use the practice tests. The guide has both sample tests and practice tests.

I had my son take some of the sample tests and found there were some concepts completely foreign to him. When I looked at the answer book, I found the concepts were foreign to me as well. To get an understanding, we went to the Kumon Center the next day for a lesson from the instructor. We were pleasantly enlightened. The process wasn't hard; it was just foreign. If you don't have a learning center or a tutor to ask about a process, use the Internet. There will probably be multiple websites that can answer a question. Ask.com and google.com are good starting points.

Have your child complete the actual practice tests using the actual answer sheets where you fill in the circle with a number two pencil. Explain the rules of the test and tell him or her that each section is timed. Don't allow your child to talk to or answer anyone in the house. Explain that when the time is up, he or she has to put the pencil down or else could be disqualified from the test. It is important to go through this exercise because children are only allowed to take the test once in the same academic school year.

When I went through the practice test process with my son, I set the timer for twenty minutes. Sitting nearby as he worked, I noticed in my peripheral vision that he had his hand up. I asked him why he had his hand up. He said he had a question. I told him that during the test he cannot ask questions. Explain to your child that when taking a multiple-choice test, it is always at least possible to guess at the answer. It is better to guess and get a chance of being right than to miss the point completely.

After you conduct the test, correct it using the answer guide. Go over the test scores with your child and discuss the incorrect answers. The guide will provide explanations of why an answer is correct.

When your child takes the actual test, you will sign him or her in at the testing school and drop him or her off at the classroom with the required materials. These usually include some number two pencils and the test registration. The test results will come about a week later. They will provide a breakdown on:

- Verbal Reasoning
- Reading Comprehension
- Quantitative Reasoning
- Mathematic Achievement

The results will also provide the score based on the norms for applicants to independent schools. The results will give the percentile rank for each category and stanine analysis, which is a formula to determine the standard score of the test. There will be a section of the analysis that provides you with the number of questions answered correctly in each category. Lastly, there will be a test profile that provides information on the scoring.

If you find that you want your test results sent to another school after your child has already taken his or her test, contact the testing company, and it will send the results to the school. There may be a fee for sending the results.

PART 5

Additional Considerations When Selecting Schools

Uniforms and Daily Preparation—What Is Your Preference?

Many people have definite preferences when it comes to uniforms. If you are pro-uniforms, it may surprise you that some private schools do not use uniforms. Most of the religious-based private schools I inquired about required uniforms. Of the independent schools I researched, I found that both elementary schools I applied to for my daughter did not require uniforms. There was a 50/50 split for uniform requirements for the middle schools I researched.

Will uniforms be a part of your decision? That depends on you. Whether you choose a school that has uniforms or not, you should have a process for getting your child ready for school each day. Some people find uniforms make their lives easier. If you work outside of your home, you may only be able to wash clothes once or twice a week. Many people have to take care of household chores on the weekend. If that describes your case, try to iron as many uniforms as you can on the weekend. At night, put the ironed uniforms out so your children will have everything they need to get ready in the morning.

If your chosen school doesn't have uniforms, you still need to follow the same process of ironing and getting your child's clothes out each night; however, without uniforms there is the potential additional complication that your child will not want to wear the clothes you have selected. You can either make executive decisions yourself or consult with your child about what he or she wants to wear.

Each family is different and will find its solution. The key is to make sure things are worked out the night before school instead of the morning of school.

School Lunches—What Is Your Preference?

Many of the schools offer lunch and snacks as part of their tuition. Schools that offer lunches are aware of food allergies and are very careful to make sure your child is not given food that could cause an allergic reaction. Instead of a cafeteria, some schools have a process whereby parents provide lunch for all students once or twice a year. The concept is that each person is assigned one or two days out of the school year to send lunch for the students. Lunch can be sandwiches, pasta, or another choice. Schools will ask what you are sending in advance so that children can decide to bring a lunch or eat what is provided.

Will school-supplied lunches impact your decision? Maybe, maybe not. I am of the opinion that school-supplied lunch is a great benefit because lunch preparation and selections can take time in the morning as well. A small child who is not quite awake in the morning could put up a battle about what he or she wants for lunch. Taking a fussy child to school is not a joyous occasion. If you select a school that does not provide lunch, try to avoid the lunch battle by asking your child the night before what he or she wants for lunch the next day. Prepare as much of the lunch as possible that night, and then add the rest in the morning.

Clothing and food are obviously important to our children. They need to be comfortable in terms of what they have on their bodies and in their bellies. Whatever your preferences in clothing and food, just keep in mind that being prepared will give you better odds of getting your child to school on time.

Being on Time and Tardiness

Many private schools have stringent rules about being at school on time. When tardiness and absences occur too many times, the result can be some kind of disciplinary action. The last thing a person wants to do is be asked to leave school because of tardiness. The sooner your child learns the value of being on time to any engagement, whether it be school, parties, family gatherings, or whatever, the better off he or she will be. When parents promote timeliness in their children, it becomes a habit they will apply to their lives as adults. If your child works in a corporate environment as an adult, he or she will have a better work ethic just by the ability to show up for work and meetings on time. Being on time shows you have respect for another person's time.

Learning the importance of being on time also teaches your children that they should not allow anyone else to disrespect their time. As an adult, your son or daughter will not experience frustration after waiting for a doctor or any other professional for more than fifteen or twenty minutes. Your adult child will know he or she is valuable and will walk away from late appointments.

Transportation—How Will the Children Get Back and Forth to School?

Another item to consider is transportation. Some schools offer bus services at nearby drop points to get your children to and from school. Depending on the age of your child, this may or may not be a good option for you. A bus service, for instance, may eliminate the need for before and after care. Check the school's website or inquire during a visit about what the school offers in terms of transportation.

If you have a high school student, you may have the option of using public transportation if bus or subway service is available near your home and the school. This is a great option if you are comfortable with your child taking the bus or subway alone. It may be the case that neighbors also going to the school can ride with your child. If you use public transportation to get to work, you can ride together with your child for either part or all of the way.

Carpooling with other parents may also be an option for you. Many schools help coordinate carpools. Check with your school on its carpool options or get to know some of the other parents and find out whether they would be interested in carpooling.

Before and After Care—Do You Need It?

Before and after care options need to be considered if you work outside your home during the day. Perhaps you are able to drop your children off in the morning at their scheduled start time and go to work. Most schools have a seven- to eight-hour day, and the typical job will require an eight-hour day. If you drop your child off in time for him or her to get to school, unless you work on the same block, you will probably get to work at least thirty minutes later. If your household allows, someone else may be able to pick your child up at the end of the day; but if you are the person who picks up and drops off the child, you will need to arrange for before or after care at the school. Inquire with the school about what types of before and after care services are available and the cost. If you are awarded a grant, many schools offer a reduction on the price of before and after care.

School Information Updates

Some schools use automated tools to provide updates. If the school is opening late, closing early, or will not open for the day, you may find out through a phone call. Many schools use the One Touch system that calls all of the families at one time to let them know of any schedule changes. Some schools provide pagers to families in the event of a schedule change.

To check your child's grades, some schools use Edline, an automated system where you can get your child's latest grades for the trimester or quarter. SchoolNotes is a website used by many schools that gives parents information on upcoming projects, tests, and events. These services help to keep everyone informed of what is going on. Newsletters are also used at most schools to provide updates of events and to highlight information.

Additional Benefits—The Code of Honor

Many private schools have a "code of honor." There are words of respect and inspiration posted and understood throughout the school. Your children will learn these positive self-affirmations throughout their school life. Self-respect is a valuable gift to your child. Some schools' code of honor extends to a trust that is not known in most schools. These schools that build trust have lockers to put your books and coats in without locks. The children leave their things outside their lockers at times. The children at these schools have every confidence that their things will be where they left them when they return.

This total respect for others' things is a gift children can take with them for the rest of their lives. You will probably find that after living the code of honor, your child will not so much as borrow a comb or lotion from you without letting you know he or she wanted to borrow it.

Stay Positive—Finding the Right School Is a Labor of Love

The process of finding a new school is going to be time consuming. If you stay organized, you will save some time, but anything worth having is going to take some of your time. Taking your child to the next level in his or her education is a labor of love. If you are feeling like you want to complain about the lengthy process of finding a new school, be aware that if you call a friend or family member and actually do complain, that person may condone your every complaint. This reinforcement may have you questioning your decision to strive for a better school for your child. Just try to keep your eyes on the final goal.

The Naysayer—Mediocrity Breeds Negativity

Some friends or family members may question your decision to put your child in a new school. You may hear something like, "Our school was good enough for Jack, and he did okay," or "The schools you are looking at are too expensive," or "You will never be able to afford it," or "You will be in debt over your head trying to go to the fancier schools." Some people may tell you the school is too far away. Your family may say that if your child becomes ill, you will have too far to go to pick him or her up. Children do get ill, but most children don't get ill every day or even more than a few days out of the school year. Most schools will have a nurse on staff. If your child attends a private school, you would have sent a signed medical form that gives the school permission to administer certain medicines to your child as well as authority to take your child to the nearest hospital in the event of an emergency. Even if your child is farther away, he or she will be in good hands.

Some friends or family may also wonder whether your child will be able to fit in to the private school environment. Rest assured that children are more adaptable than adults. Most children just want to play and learn. Depending on what part of the country you live in, there may be some real concerns about race and social stature. You will need to find out how valid those concerns are through the interview process. You can also get information from the website http://yahooed.greatschools.net/modperl/parents/dc/185/ to get a parent review on the school. You are the person who needs to do the research on the school.

No matter what you decide, remember that mediocrity breeds negativity. Don't allow negativity to distract you or to rob your child of a great education and experiences outside of his or her backyard. Many private schools are making strides to provide diversity in their school population and are educating students about other cultures.

Working Outside Your Home—It Is Important to Communicate

Each person is going to have an individual experience during a school visit. No matter what the experience, if you are a parent working outside your home, your employer needs to know you are going to be taking some time off from work. I would encourage anyone who is going to be visiting various schools to keep his or her boss aware of the situation. If you don't have a good relationship with your boss, you may want to start building a better one because you will need to be late for work a few days and will need to leave early a few times, too. Save some of your time off so you can use it for these visits.

Some of you may be thinking that doing things for your family is your personal business. What you do on your time off from work is indeed your business. If, however, a person goes from showing up on time regularly and working regular hours on a consistent basis for years to taking the morning off or leaving early repeatedly over a period of a month or two, the change will be noticeable.

Share with your immediate supervisor enough information so that he or she is comfortable with your taking the necessary time off from work. You don't have to show your boss your schedule or let him or her know which school you are going to visit. Just tell your boss you are shopping for schools for your child and are going to need to come in late a few times and/or leave early a few times. This little bit of information will alleviate any tension between you and your boss. It may also build some trust.

I have a good relationship with my own manager; however, after a few late arrivals, she asked me whether I was interviewing. I laughed and said yes, but not in the way you are thinking. I told her I was interviewing for schools for my children. She understood and didn't question me further. When I made subsequent requests for time off, I would inform my manager that the leave request was for a school visit for my child. Not all manager/employee relationships involve mutual respect, but if you are going to be leaving early or arriving late, it is a good idea to form a better relationship now while you are planning for the future.

PART 6

The Financial Aid Process

Many independent schools have an endowment fund, which gives schools the opportunity to offer grant money to families that cannot afford to pay the full tuition. Most schools will offer families some endowment money if they apply for financial aid at the time they apply for school. The grant money is intended as a supplement, and the family is responsible for making up for the difference. The endowment differs from school to school. Some schools publish their average grant amount in their enrollment information.

Whether or not you will apply for grant money (financial aid) to help pay for private school will depend on your income, how many children you have applying for school, and the price of tuition. Most lower- and middle-income families will apply for grant money from the schools unless they have just received a windfall of money. If you choose to apply for grant money, the process for independent schools is friendly to parents in that you only have to complete one application. The results of your application will be sent to the schools based on what you select on the application.

The financial aid application process works similarly to the testing process. There are identification numbers for each school, which you will indicate on your application. You can apply for financial aid online or you can complete a paper application. The primary source of financial aid for independent schools is through the School and Student Services, which can be found on the NAIS website: www.nais.org/. You will need to go to the financial aid resources page and complete a Parents' Financial Statement. There is a charge for completing the form (in 2007 the cost was less than $30), and there is a charge for every school (in 2007 the cost was less than $15) to which you want the information to be sent.

There will be some cost to you, even if it is minimal. Parents applying for financial aid should look at their budget. If you don't have a budget today, start one. Take a look at your budget and see where you can cut costs. Do you have expenses that you can reduce (e.g., credit card expenses, cable television, daily Starbucks, etc.)? If so, start working on reducing or getting rid of those expenses now. Put the extra money you do not need to spend in an account so you can have some extra to put toward the new expense of school. In addition to tuition, there are other expenses you will incur for school, such as field trips and transportation. Get ahead of the game so you will have the funds available when the expense occurs. See sample budget on the next page.

Income Taxes

Before you can complete the Parents' Financial Statement, you need either to have your income tax return completed or to complete an estimated income tax. Don't let that process prevent you from applying. If you are comfortable with completing your taxes using a tax software program, then you can complete the estimated tax information using that software. The reason for completing the estimated tax is to be able to provide the NAIS with your total federal tax paid for that year. The total federal tax is not information you can obtain from your W2 form. You actually need to complete the income tax return to get that information.

If you are not comfortable with completing your own taxes, then you should go to an income tax office or an income tax accountant to have a professional complete the estimated income tax form for you. You can also consider having a friend or family member with whom you are comfortable help you complete the income tax form. The deadline for completing the Parents' Financial Statement may be prior to your receiving the W2 forms from

Sample budget				
Paid	**MONTHLY BILLS**		**Jun-07**	
PAID	TYPE OF BILL	USUAL AMOUNT	PAYMENT DUE	COMMENTS
	Mortgage or Rent	$950	10th of month	
	Home Owner's Association	$43	1st of month	
	Car Payment	$488	15th of month	
	House Phone	$68	16th of month	
	Cell Phone	$73	8th of month	
	Newspaper Bill	$5	21st of month	Due on the third month
	Car Insurance	$350	18th of month	
	Home Owner's Insurance	$55		
	Electricity	$500	21st of month	
	Cable	$84	25th of month	
	Credit Card	$270		
	Grocery	$300		
	Gas	$200		
	Water Bill	$75	every third month	
	Miscellaneous	$150		Birthday gift
	Life Insurance: Wife	$40	every third month	Paid in May
	Life Insurance: Husband	$40	every third month	Paid in April
	Security System	$40	every third month	Paid in April
	Monthly Total	$3,731.00		

your employer. If that is the case, then you will need to use the last pay stub you had for the previous year when completing the estimated income tax.

If at all possible, you should attend a financial aid seminar prior to completing the form. These seminars are hosted by the schools, and even if you haven't applied to the school hosting the seminar, another school to which you have applied will probably send you the information about the seminar. The seminar is designed to explain the process and to give you the "dos and don'ts" about completing the form. It also gives you additional information. If you have questions, this is a good place to ask. It is also a good place to hear other people's questions that you may not have considered.

Once you start completing the application, you may have additional questions. There is a toll free telephone number you can call Monday through Friday during business hours to reach representatives who are available to answer your questions.

Once you complete your Parents' Financial Statement, most schools are going to want a copy of your income tax returns, including W2s for the current year and the previous year. You will need to send copies of your actual income tax return upon completion. Because this is your financial information, I would recommend that you mail it with some type of guarantee from the Postal Service that the mail has been received. I like to use delivery confirmation, but any type of verification is good. Another suggestion is to include a cover letter (a sample letter is included on the website link) with the tax returns so a school doesn't have to take any time matching your information to the correct file.

Many schools extend the date for sending the income tax documentation until April. If you send the information in prior to the school making its application decisions, the school will probably be able to provide you with the information on the amount of grant money it can award you at the same time it accepts your child. If you wait to send the tax information, then you will have to wait for the school to make a determination on any grant money it can provide to you.

Additional Funding

Depending on your financial circumstances, it may be necessary to request additional funding beyond what is provided by School and Student Services. If that is your situation, you just need to pursue it. The NAIS website will identify additional funding in your area. For minority students, some of the more commonly known places to request financial aid are:

- The Latino Fund
- The Black Student Fund

The Latino Fund and the Black Student Fund will want some of the same information you sent to the schools: testing, transcripts, and income tax information.

You will need to wait to receive an acceptance offer with a grant offering before you begin to pursue additional funding. If the amount of the grant is not sufficient to meet your budget, let the school know you want to pursue its acceptance but that you need more financial assistance. This is not an uncommon request. The school will require additional information from you. It needs to know your monthly income minus your expenses. Be honest with the information you provide. The school will review the information and advise you of any additional funding available. Each school is different, so the approach you need to adopt depends on your experience communicating with the school. If that school cannot grant you the money you need, consider looking at some of the other foundations. For religious schools, you can contact your place of worship to find out what funding is available through them or their organizations.

Funding through Foundations

For most people, the funding received through a grant from the school will be enough to pay for school. If the funding is still not enough, then you need to look at other foundations that fund education. Find the website of your state capital and conduct a search on corporate foundations. You would need to contact the foundations of your choice for assistance with additional funding. The NAIS website also has some listings of scholarship providers. A sample letter is included in the enclosed website link on how to ask for additional assistance.

Funding through Corporations

Lastly, there are many companies willing to help fund students of all ages. If your child aspires to make a career in the arts, contact the National Endowment for the Arts or a company that has an interest in the arts. If your child aspires to be an engineer, contact companies or government agencies in the engineering field for funding. Not every company or agency will be able to provide help, but you won't know unless you ask. A sample letter is included in the enclosed website link on how to ask for additional assistance.

PART 7

The Waiting Process—
The Application File
Is Complete

So, you have been all over town and perhaps out of town looking at schools. You have contacted teachers and school offices about teacher recommendations and transcripts. You have asked your friends for referrals. You have completed the financial aid paperwork, and you have checked with all the schools to ensure that your child's file is complete. For now, the end of the process of finding a school is on hold. All that can be done is to wait for the admissions decision letters to come to your mailbox.

Let your mind focus on your next venture. You have achieved a great deal in getting through the process successfully on behalf of your child. You should feel satisfaction in your achievement. Set your thoughts on your next goal or goals. What you think about is what you bring about. You now have time on your hands you didn't have when you were shopping for information on schools and going on visits and writing letters to various people. Take this window of time and use it to serve another worthwhile purpose.

Receiving Admission Decision Letters—How to Decide on Which School to Select

The decision letters you receive will either tell you your child was accepted, placed on a waiting list, or rejected.

If your child has not been accepted, the school may or may not tell you the factors that disqualified him or her. A rejection is hard for most students and parents. When I applied to a private school for my child entering third grade, the letter we received said he was not a good fit. My family and friends were not happy with the rejection. Many people advised me I should find out why he was not a good fit.

With any admission process, there is going to be some subjectivity. If there was another child who had an edge over my child because his or her parents were associated with the school or had some kind of inside connection, I knew I didn't have control over that situation. In the case of this first rejection, my choice was not to find out the reason. I chose this option because I didn't want my child in a school for eight hours of his day if someone in that school did not want him there. So for me, the reason my child was not accepted did not matter. I also knew you cannot bully your way into a school.

Since I had that experience, I know that rejection is sometimes the best gift. My rationale for considering rejection a gift is that if my son had been accepted to that school at that time, I might not have pursued other schools more suited for him a few years later.

The Waiting List

On the more positive side, you may receive a letter stating your child was qualified and has been put on the waiting list. The letter may say something like, "Due to the limited number of openings, we cannot offer every qualified applicant a space."

A waiting list means the school had a certain number of students to whom they could offer admission. Schools know there is a good possibility that every child who was offered admission will not accept. So schools look at the qualified applicants and put the remainder of their top students in a waiting list. Schools who offer students admissions provide a deadline for enrollment. People who do not respond by the deadline are taken off the list of new students. The school will contact other students from the waiting list to offer them a place in the school.

Selection from the waiting list may depend on the composition of the class when the space becomes available. Coeducational schools may look at the ratio of boys to girls when making offers; they may also consider cultural diversity when making decisions, or they could simply be ranking by academic scores. Every school has its own process.

The Acceptance Letter

The letter we all want to see is the congratulatory letter that says a school is pleased to offer your child a place for the coming academic year. Hooray, the school said yes! The letter will state something complimentary about your child when explaining why he or she was accepted. The letter will tell you that a response is needed by a certain time. Schools want to know that you are committed to them. Again, if you do not commit, your child will probably lose his or her place.

In your quest for finding a school for your child, you may have applied to multiple schools. If your child has applied to more than one school, he or she may well get accepted to more than one. Your child may also be placed on a waiting list at one or more schools. Lastly, your child may be rejected by one or more schools. The results will depend on many factors.

Some schools are nationally known and have thousands of applicants each year. Some have local reputations and hundreds of applicants each year. If you are applying for schools at pre-kindergarten and kindergarten levels, there will probably be more spaces to be filled. If you are applying for other grades, the spaces may be limited to the size of a new class, which could be fifteen to twenty students. Knowing that schools have lots of applicants and few spaces will help you understand their decisions.

Let's say you have applied to three schools for your child and your child has been accepted to two of them. The one school that he or she has not been accepted to is his or her first choice. Think about how you are going to advise your child on the school decisions. If your child is young, the decision may not be as difficult to explain. You may tell your child that the new school he or she will be attending is school x because (you fill in the blank here).

Handling the Emotions

If your child is older and understands the school application process, you need to sit down and discuss the letters with your child. There is not one child who is going to like being rejected by his or her top choice. As an adult, it is hard to accept rejection, so bear in mind it is probably even worse for a child. Take the time with your child to discuss the rejection and the associated feelings. Your family will not be able to make a good choice from the other options until you work through those feelings.

Decision Tree—Removing Some of the Subjectivity

Once the emotions have been addressed and worked out, a part of your decision about choosing the right school will be intuitive. You can make your selection of the school of your choice less subjective by using a chart to grade various qualities about each possibility to help you decide. Rank each item from 1 to 5, with 5 being the highest ranking and 1 the lowest. Total each school's score at the end, and you will find your best choices. Your child can be a part of the ranking process. See the chart below. A sample chart with more variety is included in the website link.

School Name	Technology	Location & Transportation	Language Offered	Uniforms	Food	Sports	Total
School A	3	4	4	5	5	5	26
School B	5	3	4	4	5	5	26
School C	3	3	3	3	1	2	15
School D	4	2	4	4	5	5	24
School E	4	2	3	4	5	5	23
School F	5	4	5	3	5	5	27
School G	5	4	5	5	4	5	28

Sample chart to rank schools

Based on your totals, you can eliminate the schools with the lowest scores. If you know you are not going to select any particular schools, as soon as you possibly can, take the time to respond to those schools in writing with your decision. This will give them an opportunity to accept another child.

Once you narrow your choices down to a handful of schools, you and your child may want to take the time on a weekend to visit those schools and get a feel for what seems right for you. Seeing a school again can help with making the final decision. If your child has not had an opportunity for a shadow day visit, call the school and schedule a shadow day. If uniforms are required at the school, have your child dress as closely as possible to the uniform so he or she can fit in. If you need to use the school's transportation service, ask the school to allow your child to ride the bus for the shadow day. You want your child to feel comfortable about his or her new school.

Read Your Contract Carefully

Before you sign on the line, read your contract carefully: It states that you are 100 percent committed to the school in terms of the tuition minus any financial aid. This commitment means you are obligated to pay the tuition even if you decide to remove your child from the school during the school year. Some schools will offer a tuition refund plan in the event your child is dismissed or you withdraw him or her from the school. There will be a cost to the tuition refund plan, but it will be minimal by comparison with the amount you would have to pay if you could not keep the commitment of enrolling your child for the full school year.

In addition, there may be other costs involved. Examples are tutoring, music lessons, field trips, and parent associations. If you are not sure about any part of the contract, contact the school's financial aid office to get clarity on the issue before you sign.

Homework—Setting Goals

Even though your child is moving on in the next few months, he or she still needs to stay connected to the current school. In addition, let your child know he or she needs to maintain or improve grades for the remainder of the year. The new school will require academic transcripts for the current school year as well as test scores.

Children should have good feelings about their new school. Tell your child to hold onto those good feelings and think about goals for the future. Ask your child to visualize the future. Let your child know that his or her visualization will come to fruition if he or she believes it can. Emphasize what your child has gained from his or her current school. Children need to learn early in life not to burn bridges.

Tell your child to decide what he or she wants from the new school and to pursue his or her goals. Let your child know that whatever good experiences come his or her way are richly deserved. I hope your child will express gratitude for the opportunity to go to a new school. Let you child know the gratitude you feel for his or her positive and active participation in the process.

Lastly, give your child an assignment. Ask him or her to write down goals for the next two weeks after you have decided on a school, so you both will have something concrete to refer to. A goal is simply a plan. If you haven't discussed setting goals with your child, find a time to discuss goals. Goals bring hope to a person's mind. Your child knows he or she will be attending a new school next year but might not know yet what that will really mean. Helping your child to set goals will allow him or her to embrace what is to come and to see the future in a new school.

Follow-Up

Some "To Dos"

Your tasks are never ending when it comes to your child. You will need to contact your present school at the end of the school year to request that the final report card and transcript be sent to the new school. Check the website of the new school to keep up with events prior to the end of the current school year, such as parent welcoming events. If you are considering putting your child in summer camp at the new school, you will want to follow-up with the school on registration deadlines. If summer reading assignments are a part of the new school, find out when the list will be generated so you can secure a copy from the library or bookstore. Lastly, keep track of the events coming up prior to the start of the school year since dates may differ from those of your current school.

Upon the start of the new school year for your child, you will need to focus on your child's school-work, activities, and disposition. Check with your child often to make sure he or she is making the adjustment to a new environment. Constant evaluation will be needed to make sure the new school is a good match for your child. If he or she is struggling socially or academically, work with the school to make any necessary adjustments. As with any change, there may need to be adjustments, as children don't always know how to fit in.

If you find the new school is not a good fit for your child and have exhausted all avenues to make the transition, all is not yet lost. Start the process again. Think through the qualities you wanted. If something has changed, change with it. Make the adjustment. You have been through the process once, so you can do it again.

On the positive side, I hope the new school you have found for your child is the perfect fit and that you will be able to remain at the new school until your child moves to the next level. Keep the entry-level years in mind when it is time to move on. Good luck to you and your family. If you keep your goals in mind, you can move mountains.

RECOMMENDED READING FOR TEENS

Cashflow Quadrant: Rich Dad's Guide to Financial Freedom, Robert T. Kiyosaki with Sharon L. Lechter, C.P.A.

Chicken Soup for the Teenage Soul, Jack Canfield, Mark Victor Hansen, and Kimberly Kirberger

Fiske Guide to Getting into the Right College, Edward B. Fiske and Bruce G. Hammond

Making College Count, Patrick S. O'Brien

The Measure of Our Success, Marian Wright Edelman

Rich Dad Poor Dad for Teens: The Secrets About Money—That You Don't Learn in School!, Robert T. Kiyosaki with Sharon L. Lechter, C.P.A.

The Seven Habits of Highly Effective Teens, Sean Covey

Who Moved My Cheese? For Teens, Spencer Johnson, M.D.

INDEX

ABOUT THE AUTHOR

Sandra L. Frazier is a corporate systems manager for an insurance company with more than seven years' project management experience. She graduated from the University of Maryland and received an Associate's Certificate in project management from ESI International. Sandra researched private schools extensively while deciding where to send her own son and daughter and is now sharing her findings with others who also want to pursue the best possible educations for their children. *Private School—It's Not Just for the Wealthy Anymore* is her first book.

Give the Gift of

Private School—
It's Not Just for the Wealthy Anymore

A Parent's Guide to Getting Your Child Accepted into Private School

to Your Friends and Colleagues

CHECK YOUR LEADING BOOKSTORE OR ORDER HERE

❑ **YES**, I want _______ copies of *Private School—It's Not Just for the Wealthy Anymore* at $14.95 each, plus $4.95 shipping per book (Maryland residents please add .75 sales tax per book). Canadian orders must be accompanied by a postal money order in U.S. funds. Allow 15 days for delivery.

❑ **YES**, I am interested in having Sandra L. Frazier speak or give a seminar to my company, association, school, or organization. Please send information.

My check or money order for $___________ is enclosed.

Please charge my: ❑ Visa   ❑ MasterCard
                   ❑ Discover   ❑ American Express

Name ____

Organization ____

Address ____

City/State/Zip ____

Phone___________________________ Email ___________________

Card # ____

Exp. Date________________ Signature ________________________

Please make your check payable and return to:

A Better Tomorrow Publishing

P.O. Box 2975 • Upper Marlboro, MD 20773-2975

Call your credit card order to: 1-866-980-8541

Fax: (301) 576-8070   www.abettertomorrowpublishing.net